Anxiety

Addressing Cognitive Overprocessing And Negative Emotional Patterns In Interpersonal Connections

(Strategies For Combating And Conquering Anxiety Through Cognitive Restructuring)

Ghislain Boily

TABLE OF CONTENT

Managing Expectations And Building From There 1

Social Anxiety in Young People 6

The Value of Social Interaction 51

Magical Pathways to Joy 69

Being able to read people 89

The Knowledge Acquired in Cognitive Behavioral Therapy 101

An Exposition on the Biological Mechanisms Underlying Stress 106

How to Handle Negative Emotions 119

Medical Conditions Which Contribute to the Development of Anxiety 131

Managing Expectations And Building From There

If you are afflicted by severe anxiety that has a substantial impact on your quality of life, it is advisable to exercise caution and refrain from immersing yourself abruptly into exceedingly demanding circumstances. Assuming you were a professional fighter, and your track record only consisted of a handful of victories. Surely, one would not desire to engage in combat with an individual who holds the prestigious title of champion and maintains an impeccable record of never having been defeated, would one? One must approach the task of conquering anxiety in a similar manner. In the realm of professional combat sports, a trainer typically seeks out bouts against adversaries whom they are aware that their fighter stands a favorable likelihood of prevailing against. The trainer will utilize these matches to obtain feedback regarding the strengths and weaknesses exhibited by their fighter. Subsequently, they will seize this opportunity to either address those weaknesses effectively or enhance the capabilities of the fighter in specific domains. Once they had achieved several victories, they would subsequently seek to challenge more formidable adversaries. The upcoming opponent would present a greater challenge, as the fighter's consistent victories against opponents who were possibly of average or slightly below-average skill have bolstered their confidence. This procedure is iterated until the pugilist has amassed a satisfactory level of self-assurance to confront an opponent for whom a victory would be deemed the pinnacle of their professional trajectory. Anxiety must be addressed in a similar manner. While it may not always be feasible to evade circumstances that induce anxiety, it is possible to perceive them as opportunities to acquire significant insight into oneself and develop a comprehensive understanding of areas necessitating personal improvement, ultimately regaining control over one's life. Many individuals often hold themselves to unreasonably high standards. There is no inherent fault in setting ambitious goals, however, if historical evidence does not suggest a probable likelihood of success in a given circumstance, it is expected that one may experience feelings of anxiety. Your current state defines who you are, and it is essential for you to prioritize the development of strategies and plans that take into account these circumstances, particularly with regard to anxiety management and confidence building. For example, if you lack proficiency in engaging in social interactions, that is your current disposition. Should I express my intention to engage in conversations, I anticipate a resurgence of apprehension and unease. However, I can direct my attention towards actively listening and deriving inspiration from the other person's enthusiasm, while also engaging in thoughtful dialogue by asking relevant inquiries. Subsequently, opportunities may arise wherein I can contribute beneficial insights to the conversation. We do not imply that one should possess low aspirations or adopt unambitious goals in relation to their desires or endeavors. If the objective is to earn one million dollars within a year, then that is acceptable. Nevertheless, you would have established exceptionally lofty standards, the attainment of which would position you among the esteemed ranks of the elite. Are you capable of meeting the expectations at this level? Are you susceptible to succumbing to the demands placed upon you? Would you be able to progress beyond mere contemplation and engage in profound reflective thinking to develop a robust strategy? Appropriate handling of expectations is crucial as it mitigates the potential consequences of anxiety, fear, and doubt that are otherwise associated with inadequately managed expectations. It is essential to grasp the concept that acquiring the knowledge of effectively positioning oneself for success in a specific situation can serve as a crucial factor in surmounting anxiety and ultimately realizing one's innate potential. Effort is required; however, we are dedicated to assisting you in your journey. The subsequent two chapters will center around distinct strategies one can employ to actively combat anxiety and cultivate confidence, presented in a concise and organized bullet point structure.

Social Anxiety in Young People

Social anxiety disorders are not solely restricted to adults; they can also afflict children. Children afflicted by social anxiety and phobia primarily experience a fear of being subjected to criticism. One manner in which they typically articulate such distress is by inquiring, for instance:

What if I were to engage in foolish actions or utterances?

- In the event that I speak or behave inappropriately...

A different manner in which young children articulate their social anxiety and phobia is through the manifestation of tears and tantrums when confronted with intimidating circumstances. Unfortunately, these particular actions are frequently misjudged as obstinacy or, even worse, the consequence of indulgent upbringing. The apprehension that instigates such conduct can lead to the manifestation of social anxiety symptoms, such as respiratory distress, perspiration, and tremors. Additionally, these symptoms have the potential to disrupt their regular, everyday routines as they may manifest well in advance of the imminent situation or triggering event. The level of apprehension experienced by children with social anxiety is frequently exaggerated when compared to the actual event and its outcomes.

Social anxiety may originate within the confines of one's household and subsequently manifest in various domains of a child's existence, including educational settings. Research has revealed that the caliber of time devoted to engaging with one's children carries greater significance compared to the sheer amount of time allocated. It is imperative that children are made aware of the presence of love, their own inherent beauty, as well as their capacity to confront the challenges of the world. It is the responsibility of a parent to provide their child with the necessary knowledge to confront the difficulties they may encounter in life, and this encompasses imparting skills for effectively managing uncomfortable social situations. Socially isolating your child and refraining from engaging in group activities with them significantly contributes to initiating a progression towards Social Anxiety Disorder (SAD). Active participation in your child's life will greatly contribute to their overall development.

Performance And Interaction

Regarding social anxiety in children, there exist two primary forms: performance anxiety and interaction anxiety.

Children may potentially encounter episodes of social anxiety when faced with situations such as placing orders at dining establishments, delivering speeches in a classroom setting, purchasing confectionery from stores, and even participating in prayer in front of a small gathering. These events or activities pertain to actions or engagements, concerning individuals stricken with social anxiety. They harbor apprehensions over potential judgment, ridicule, or humiliation resulting from even the slightest of errors or blunders.

Performance anxiety tends to be particularly magnified in children who are burdened with overzealous parents who possess meticulous expectations of flawlessness. If an individual imposes excessively rigid guidelines upon their child, to the extent that the child's performance inherently fails to measure up, it effectively creates a situation where the child's potential for success is impeded, leaving them devoid of opportunities for achievement.

Children may also encounter episodes of social anxiety precipitated by mere proximity to other individuals - engaging in social interaction with them. Some instances that may trigger the condition include utilizing a communal lavatory, visiting an amusement center, partaking in a celebratory gathering, engaging in religious practices, availing medical services, accessing medical facilities, and participating in familial gatherings, among various other scenarios. Frequently, it can be observed that children afflicted with interactional social anxiety commonly experience concomitant performance social anxiety as well. Insufficient provision of social interaction opportunities during early childhood may result in the child experiencing discomfort and unease in subsequent social events.

What is the mechanism through which children acquire it?

A potential cause of social anxiety in children is genetic predisposition, as it has a hereditary component. It is noted to be more prevalent among children with a parental or other first-degree familial presence of the disorder. There are instances, nevertheless, in which the cause is attributed to environmental factors as opposed to genetic inheritance. There exists a robust correlation, however, genetics cannot be regarded as the sole determinant.

Children may also be affected by it through firsthand exposure. A child who might have undergone a distressing social encounter could potentially manifest symptoms indicative of social anxiety disorder. Consider, for instance, the case of children who experience bullying within the educational setting. Given that bullying is a communal occurrence, frequently unfolding in the presence of numerous peers, the resulting humiliated encounter can profoundly affect a child's psychological well-being and instill within them a tendency to associate such experiences with socializing among their peers. It is possible that there is a genetic component to the social anxiety, with the manifestation being elicited by a traumatic incident, thus representing a confluence of both factors.

Understanding Negative Attachment

The phrase emotional baggage tends to be frequently employed, although it is not devoid of validity. The associations we establish are never completely liberated from our initial relationship encounters. Frequently, individuals may employ phrases such as "she harbors unresolved paternal concerns" or "he grapples with unresolved maternal concerns." All of these indications imply that our capacity to connect and establish connections with others is fundamentally shaped by the quality of our past interpersonal relationships.

An enduring connection established during childhood shall impart essential principles for fostering integrity in any relationship. Parents who provide a nurturing environment are more inclined to enhance the emotional well-being of their children compared to parents who are abusive or emotionally unavailable. In the event that your parents consistently provided unwavering support, nurtured your development, and fostered a sense of security, it is probable that you will develop a propensity for placing trust in others as you age. You will develop a strong sense of self-worth and cultivate secure emotional bonds, enabling you to establish profound interpersonal connections.

Now consider the scenario of an individual who was raised in a family characterized by abusive dynamics. Their parents rarely acknowledged their needs, and they lacked someone whom they could confide in. In this particular circumstance, the child acquires adaptive strategies to endure their adverse living conditions.

These coping mechanisms may include the acquisition of emotional suppression skills, employing attention-seeking tactics towards their parents, or even resorting to truancy during academic sessions. This child develops trust issues, struggles to express emotions, and, perhaps most detrimentally, possesses a diminished sense of self-value.

Evidently, there exists a stark contrast between these two individuals in terms of their approach to establishing connections with individuals in the context of both romantic relationships and life in general. Although it is feasible to overcome the effects of childhood trauma, the majority of individuals do not possess a complete understanding of their own emotional condition. This implies that you may possess a limited comprehension of the underlying factors that contribute to your feelings of insecurity or anxiety within interpersonal connections. As you seem to lack awareness regarding the emotional burdens you carry, you continuously transition from one relationship to another, yet the underlying problems persist.

Do you often find yourself desiring to establish intimacy with another person, yet simultaneously harboring apprehension that drawing too near might result in emotional harm? Do you typically experience feelings of apprehension regarding the potential departure of your partner, or consistently harbor doubts about their level of appreciation for you? Do you frequently experience apprehension regarding the possibility of committing errors or making inappropriate remarks? These characteristics signify adverse attachment patterns within relationships.

Jack exhibits characteristics of a caring and dedicated father. Additionally, he thoroughly enjoys engaging in quality bonding moments with his family. Every day, he ensures to carve out time from his schedule to be with his wife and children. However, lately, he has noticed a sense of emotional detachment growing between him and his wife. He ponders if she is engaged in an extramarital relationship or if her disinterest towards him has grown.

Recently, he has begun accessing her Facebook and other social media platforms for the sole purpose of ensuring that she is not engaging in any infidelity. He is aware that such actions frequently constitute a significant violation of her privacy, yet persists in engaging in them nonetheless. Although his wife may be unaware of his transgressions, she is becoming progressively disinterested in his dependency. Occasionally, she desires a brief respite in solitude to relax, yet Jack appears incapable of granting her the necessary personal space.

She anticipates the opportunity to depart from her residence and alleviate the stress encountered there. Her familial members have observed that she has begun allocating an increased amount of time during the weekends to engage in activities with her parents. According to her, this frequently occurs due to the children's longing for their grandparents. However, on a deeper level, she acknowledges that it is primarily driven by her own need for distance from Jack.

Although it cannot be definitively concluded that Jack's wife is engaging in infidelity, it is evident that she is increasingly seeking solace in being distant from him. This frequently serves as a prototypical illustration of the detrimental impact that negative attachment has on relationships. Similar to Jack, the majority of individuals characterized by negative attachment patterns rely heavily on consistent reassurance from their partners. They are of the opinion that they constantly require validation from their partner. At the outset, the partner may perceive this ongoing requirement for reassurance as charming and even captivating; however, over time, they start to experience a sense of constraint and restriction.

When harboring negative sentiments towards someone, your state of happiness or lack thereof is contingent upon the actions or presence of that individual. You desire for them to experience a sense of validation and worthiness. Their emotional state has an immediate impact on your own disposition. You consistently prioritize their happiness, even at the expense of your own needs. Gradually, this deleterious dynamic commences to taint the bond. One becomes disinterested in relinquishing their own needs to maintain the contentment of the other party. You exhibit irritability, anger, and a tendency to experience emotional outbursts.

Your counterpart, however, becomes disinterested in assuming emotional responsibility for you. They develop a growing desire for independence and gradually commence disengaging from the relationship. Whilst you endeavor to maintain the bond, your partner is equally exerting efforts to disengage. As a consequence, your anxiety progressively influences both your psychological state and behavioral patterns.

Individuals who possess adverse emotional attachment tend to experience heightened levels of anxiety within their relationships, primarily stemming from a deep-seated fear of being abandoned. This fear commonly originates from childhood experiences. Studies have revealed that individuals who have experienced adverse familial circumstances during childhood have an increased propensity to develop detrimental attachment patterns in adulthood. This is due to their lack of awareness regarding the dynamics of healthy relationships and the experience of being unconditionally loved by others.

The presence of apprehension leading to adverse bonding commonly stems from the anxiety of not attaining a state of well-being. A deficiency in positive self-regard gives rise to the emergence of adverse emotional connections. When one reaches the point of believing that they are unworthy of love, it becomes difficult for them to conceive that their partner will hold them in high regard.

This generates a state of anxiety that prompts a perpetual yearning for validation and reassurance.

Individuals who possess an adverse attachment style tend to perceive relationships as a means to discover themselves or address a void within their existence. Regrettably, a mutually beneficial relationship can only be established when both individuals involved maintain a sense of equality and avoid dependence on one another. Negative attachments in relationships can facilitate the formation of toxic relationships, codependent relationships, and situations of narcissistic abuse.

Behavioral Approach Test

Therapists occasionally employ a method known as the behavioral approach test (BAT) in order to facilitate the recognition of physical, cognitive, and behavioral manifestations of anxiety. Utilizing this approach, one would actively expose themselves to a situation that elicits fear, followed by promptly recording their anxious symptoms and behaviors.

Anne's therapist made the request for her to commence her workday at 8:00 a.m., deviating from her accustomed routine of starting at 7:30 a.m., in order to facilitate the observation of her anxious response. There was still ample time to arrive by 9:00 a.m., which coincided with her designated commencement. Upon her arrival at the workplace, Anne proceeded to make a written record of the sensations she experienced earlier in the morning, as a result of departing at a later hour. She observed that her physique was experiencing heightened muscle tension and she harbored concerns regarding punctuality in reaching her workplace. She had telephoned her spouse seeking solace, and upon her arrival at the workplace, a headache had commenced. She experienced such a heightened level of anxiety that she found it necessary to take a brief respite in the women's restroom before proceeding to her workstation. She assigned a rating of 10 to her anxiety level upon commencing her work.

In certain instances, confronting a situation that is feared may elicit excessive levels of anxiety. Alternatively, your therapist would employ a role-playing technique for the purpose of evaluating your anxiety. In Anne's situation, her therapist and she would simulate her morning routine, including her departure for work at a later hour. Additionally, this would afford the therapist the opportunity to directly observe her subsequent anxious response within the envisaged scenario.

If you are experiencing difficulty in recognizing your anxiety symptoms, we recommend undertaking an individual behavioral approach assessment as a means of clarification. Engage in an apprehensive scenario where you possess a sense of fear, subsequently documenting your emotional distress, cognitive processes, and corresponding actions. If that appears excessively challenging, engage in a simulated enactment where you envision yourself embarking on the given situation. Please record any observations you may have regarding this exercise in the designated area provided.

SAFETY BEHAVIORS

When faced with perceived threats, it is possible that individuals may resort to employing safety behaviors as a means of alleviating fear and anxiety. While engaging in these behaviors provides temporary relief from anxiety, they ultimately extend its duration in the long run. For instance, if an individual were to have social anxiety disorder, they may mitigate their anxiety by refraining from expressing their viewpoint. By adopting such an approach, you come to realize that maintaining silence is the sole means to navigate social circumstances. You never get the chance to test out that belief—and discover whether it could be wrong. Safety behaviors may manifest in overt or inconspicuous forms; several instances are enumerated as follows.

Refraining from circumstances such as remaining indoors.

Requiring the presence of a reliable confidant to provide assistance in the event of a panic attack.

Seeking an early departure from social gatherings that induce feelings of anxiety or discomfort.

Subtle behaviors such as glancing at a mobile device or excessively practicing a presentation

Persistently seeking validation and confirmation from others

Engaging in a form of cognitive diversion from an intimidating circumstance, such as immersing oneself in literature prior to a public speaking engagement.

Engaging in behavioral adaptations in order to minimize the impact of anxiety, such as averting gaze while receiving an injection or firmly gripping a handrail in a lofty location.

Vigilantly observing your physical symptoms with the intention of managing them.

Anxiety Triggers

In instances of uncertainty, Anne experienced feelings of anxiety and distress. The uncertainty of traffic conditions on the freeway, the lack of clarity regarding her supervisor's satisfaction with her efforts, and the prospect of her family members falling ill caused her sleep deprivation. It appeared that she possessed the ability to be concerned about nearly everything. She was concerned about present circumstances, such as the ability to meet their financial obligations, as well as hypothetical scenarios, for instance, the potential diagnosis of an untreatable ailment.

Gaining insight into the specific factors that elicit your anxiety—the circumstances that give rise to your manifestation of anxiety—is a fundamental aspect of strategizing treatment. Although certain instances of your anxiety may appear to lack a direct cause and be unrelated to any specific trigger, it is probable that some of your symptoms manifest consistently.

When it comes to specific phobias, it is typically straightforward to ascertain the causative factors of anxiety. If one experiences acrophobia, they are likely to experience feelings of anxiety when occupying a high floor of a building. If one experiences a fear of needles, they are likely to experience a growing sense of panic as they await the administration of a flu shot.

An array of social and performance situations can instigate social anxiety disorder. Engaging in conversations with unfamiliar individuals, encountering novel acquaintances, extending inquiries for social engagements, articulating personal viewpoints, or partaking in employment assessments are frequently encountered scenarios that can elicit anxiety. Common stimulants of performance anxiety encompass activities such as consuming food or beverages in the presence of others, engaging in written tasks in public view, delivering speeches to an audience, and utilizing communal restroom facilities.

Regarding panic disorder, the instigators of distress encompass physiological sensations and the subsequent perception of said sensations. Individuals with panic disorder often possess heightened sensitivity to bodily sensations, leading them to interpret and perceive such signals in an exaggeratedly catastrophic manner. Chest discomfort is perceived as indicative of a myocardial infarction. The experience of experiencing difficulty in breathing transitions into the state of hyperventilation. The apprehension stemming from the interpretation of physical symptoms as indicative of an underlying medical condition is frequently observed as a catalyst for panic disorder.

If an individual experiences agoraphobia, their anxiety is typically elicited by situations where they perceive that escape would be challenging in the event of a panic attack. Such situations include using public transportation, being present in expansive or enclosed spaces, navigating through crowds or queues, and being outside their residence unaccompanied.

What circumstances or entities elicit trepidation or prompt you to abstain?

What particular characteristics of these objects or scenarios exacerbate your anxiety? Can you recall the initial instance when you experienced significant distress or endured an episode of anxiety? Consider the events unfolding at the given moment, as well as any distinctive characteristics associated with the circumstances. Please document your recollections in the designated area provided.

Evolutionary

Evolutionary influences might also contribute to the development of social anxiety disorder. In order to comprehend this concept, it is crucial to bear in mind that humans are an inherently social species, thus finding pleasure and fulfillment in the company of others. Certain individuals may have an aversion to the notion of causing distress to others and fear the potential consequences of social rejection. Consequently, for a subset of people, the emergence of a social anxiety disorder can be attributed to an inherent propensity for heightened sensitivity towards unfavorable judgments. This may be the reason why a significant number of individuals experiencing social anxiety engage in behavior that intentionally disrupts others, ultimately leading to detrimental consequences for themselves in the long run.

Biological

Additionally, it has been proposed that social anxiety disorder may be linked to familial associations. Examine your ancestral lineage – should any individual within your family exhibit tendencies of social anxiety, it is highly probable that you may acquire similar disposition through inheritance of their character. Although a distinct correlation has been observed indicating a tendency for anxiety disorders to manifest within familial relations, the precise causative factor remains uncertain. This ambiguity arises as it remains unclear whether these disorders arise from genetic predispositions or if children acquire them as a result of witnessing and emulating their parents' anxious behaviors. Nevertheless, it is plausible that the genetic composition could exert a more significant influence on rates of social anxiety than is presently understood. Ongoing research is being conducted in this domain.

Negative or adverse encounters.

When an individual undergoes an unfavorable or traumatic event, they may experience profound distress in the immediate aftermath. However, the impact of that experience on an individual goes beyond its initial occurrence. A selection of frequently reported experiences, pertaining specifically to individuals who exhibit social anxiety, often trace their origins back to their academic years. Bullying exemplifies the phenomenon, along with any discriminatory treatment that marginalizes individuals as peculiar, somewhat deviant, and unwelcome in the perception of others; all of these factors can significantly contribute to the development of social anxiety persisting throughout one's lifespan.

Post-traumatic stress disorder (PTSD) is frequently observed as a notable outcome of acute traumatic incidents, exacerbating pre-existing social anxiety disorders. Continually dwelling on past painful encounters via flashbacks perpetuates the prominence of pessimistic thoughts in your consciousness, preventing you from approaching social scenarios with impartiality.

The Expectations of Existence

When engaging in conversation with individuals who are diagnosed with social anxiety disorder, the majority of them tend to express an enduring presence of the condition, while a subset report its onset during their teenage years or early twenties. Adolescents and young individuals encounter numerous challenges, particularly in the realm of social interaction, as they embark on the journey towards independence and strive to fulfill society's expectations of adulthood.

Public schools provide a multitude of occasions and circumstances that may lead to social discomfort and uneasiness. Effectively navigating these circumstances in order to prevent the development of Social Anxiety Disorder necessitates substantial guidance and open dialogue. Overcoming these challenges is undeniably arduous, and the patterns forged by these young adults may exert a lasting influence on their future trajectories, rendering certain aspects of life increasingly formidable to navigate. A multitude of secondary education students commence their collegiate journey grappling with the challenge of assimilation, investing substantial efforts in attempting to make a favorable impression on their peers, both in terms of appearance and intellectual prowess.

The Challenges of the Current Era

There exist two forms of stress that are liable to impact the degree of anxiety experienced by an individual - substantial relocations leading to the severance of connections with colleagues, friends, and/or family; and notable alterations that influence one's interpersonal dynamics, such as a shift in their occupational role. These requirements necessitate swift adaptation to new circumstances and consume a considerable amount of energy, with minimal likelihood of having any surplus.

Engaging in any circumstance that entails encountering unfamiliar individuals and establishing fresh connections is inherently burdensome, as one must navigate this uncharted territory, acquaint oneself with the other party, and simultaneously project a favorable impression. There exists a notable expectation to make a lasting impression, and the apprehension of not meeting expectations can induce substantial unease. Confidence must be developed, and during this period, it is probable that former vulnerabilities will emerge.

Technology

The prevalence of social anxiety disorder, alongside several other anxiety disorders, is increasing. An increasing number of individuals in contemporary society appear to be experiencing a disconnection and encountering challenges in their pursuit of harmonious coexistence within the global community. Encounters of depression have witnessed a rising trend, with anxiety disorders serving as just one aspect of the broader association with depression. A significant portion (50%) of individuals who receive a diagnosis of depression also experience symptoms of anxiety, and conversely, an equivalent proportion of individuals diagnosed with anxiety also exhibit signs of depression. Antidepressants rank as the second most commonly prescribed medications in the United States, while the rates of suicide have been consistently increasing annually.

Having examined the impact of genetics, hormonal discrepancies, and environmental factors on anxiety disorders, it is imperative to consider another pivotal element: technology.

The feeling of loneliness is huge among people suffering from SAD and depression. The advancements in technology have bestowed upon us the capacity to foster greater connectivity while simultaneously deepening our sense of loneliness. But how can such an occurrence be explained? Let us now examine the case of Greenland.

Presently, Greenland exhibits one of the most elevated rates of suicide globally. Nevertheless, this phenomenon did not transpire until the consolidation of small villages into desolate areas, as a consequence of the populace seeking employment and educational opportunities in the capital. One might assume that individuals residing within a sizable community would experience reduced feelings of isolation and despondency in comparison to those living in a small village comprising merely 50 inhabitants. Nevertheless, as proximity grew closer, Greenland encountered a decline in its communal spirit. An individual's level of anxiety or depression is not exclusively contingent upon the presence or absence of other individuals in their vicinity. It is a universally acknowledged truth that one has the potential to experience profound loneliness even in the midst of a gathering of individuals. As individuals, our nature as humans is inherently social, and in the absence of a supportive community, we may experience a sense of existential void.

Technology has, to a certain extent, exerted a comparable influence in the United States as the centralization of jobs and education has done in Greenland. Access to communication with a vast multitude, spanning thousands or even millions, lies at our very fingertips. However, it is a rarity to witness these interactions delve beyond superficiality and cultivate meaningful connections. Due to our increased reliance on screens, we have inadvertently neglected the art of face-to-face interactions. Consequently, a significant number of individuals experience apprehension in social settings where their actions are observed directly, as opposed to being perceived solely through textual information on a digital platform.

Technology is indeed a commendable instrument, yet rather than employing it as a carpenter utilizes a saw, we have allowed ourselves to be wielded by its influence. Has anyone ever encountered a scenario where a carpenter utilizes a saw? Nobody. It does not function in that manner. However, we find ourselves continually tethered to electronic devices, allowing them to exert control over every facet of our existence. If one discovers that they tend to allocate a greater amount of time to screen-related activities rather than engaging in face-to-face interactions within their physical surroundings, this could potentially be identified as a contributing factor to the development of Seasonal Affective Disorder.

Should you encounter this issue, it may be necessary for you to acquire the skill of managing and restricting the amount of time you spend using electronic devices. One potential option would be to consider configuring your smartphone to terminate data reception once a specified limit is reached. Alternatively, it may be worth contemplating reverting to a basic mobile phone until you believe you are capable of managing it more effectively.

It is possible that you might also perceive your circle of acquaintances as failing to foster a sense of community. It is plausible that you experience a perpetual sense of judgment due to the association you maintain with individuals who exhibit a propensity for making critical assessments. If you consistently encounter persistent criticism whenever you socialize with your friends, it is unsurprising that you encounter feelings of anxiety. It may be opportune to seek out alternative companions. As previously stated, there are numerous support groups available for individuals afflicted by SAD, which can serve as a valuable community wherein you can discover a sense of purpose.

In contemporary times, there is a tendency to readily dismiss traditions and religious beliefs on the grounds that they appear to be antiquated superstitious notions that no longer align with prevailing scientific knowledge. Nevertheless, the legacy and customs of your culture may hold greater significance than you may perceive. Cicero's renowned words capture this sentiment: "Those who are unaware of the events preceding their own existence are destined to perpetually dwell in a state of immaturity." What is the value of the human existence if it is not intricately entwined with the lives of our forefathers, as chronicled in historical accounts? Absent a guiding compass, we are mere vessels adrift in the vast ocean, at the mercy of whichever wave propels us. It is comprehensible that residing in this fashion gives rise to a considerable degree of apprehension.

Day 3

Exercise:

Please transcribe all the designations and descriptive terms that you and others employ to define your identity onto a sheet of paper.

For instance, do you perceive yourself in the roles of a son, daughter, mother, father, student, educator, cashier, companion, engineer, accountant, employee, employer, roommate, spouse, etcetera? And which descriptive terms do you employ to define your personal identity? For instance, do you associate yourself with concepts such as unsuccessful, accomplished, content, despondent, virtuous, immoral, desirous, avaricious, precious, or insignificant? Not only should you record the labels and descriptions you perceive, but you should also document your assumptions about how others perceive you. Consider whether you believe others view you as a valuable companion, an unintelligent and inept employee, an exceptionally intelligent and skilled worker, and so on. Please take as much time as necessary to complete the task at hand, ensuring that you fill an entire sheet of paper with the necessary labels and corresponding descriptions.

Once you have completed the task, proceed to tear the paper into numerous fragments and dispose of them appropriately. Those labels and adjectives carry no significance or weight. They're not you. One's identity defies limitations imposed by titles, rendering them ineffective in capturing, categorizing, elucidating, or dictating one's essence. The majority of individuals contaminate their moral compass by employing such acquired lexicon. They possess a deep conviction in the profound influence of these utterances - to such an extent that they are willing to engage in combat, endure tremendous distress, suffer from ailments, and even face death in order to manifest these words into existence. Anxiety, along with the majority of societal circumstances, instills in you the practice of aligning oneself with specific words, which essentially amount to mere thoughts. Unlearn them.

Engaging in 10 minutes of peaceful silence and deliberate deep breathing. Recite the phrase: "I do not identify myself solely based on labels, titles, or descriptions."

Please utilize the hashtag #30DaysIdentity to share this personal encounter.

Day 4

Exercise:

Proceed to incrementally count up to the number 25 at a leisurely pace, taking brief pauses in between each number. Subsequently, commence with the gradual enumeration in reverse order starting from 25. Attempt this task while your eyes remain shut. During the process of incrementing the count, one can envision oneself being elevated into the celestial expanse, and subsequently, in the event of decrementing the count, descending back to the terrestrial realm.

The contemporary world is characterized by a pervasive emphasis on rapidity. Many individuals appear to be in a state of haste, yet the majority of them express discontentment and lack direction in their pursuits. The pursuit of incessantly seeking the next best thing is a futile undertaking. Only a select few individuals possess the ability to appreciate and savor the present moment, irrespective of its characteristics. Due to the abundance of issues and the primary focus of most occupations on addressing these concerns, individuals are compelled to embrace feelings of anxiety as they hasten towards achieving desired outcomes and resolutions. That surely isn't happiness. Genuine happiness can solely be discovered within the confines of the present moment, rather than within the realms of a potential future characterized by achievements and rewards. Hastiness is tantamount to making no progress.

To what extent have you hurriedly engaged in the processes of critical thinking and problem-solving? This has a detrimental impact on both your mental well-being and physical health, leading to impaired concentration, increased stress levels, and an inability to remain fully mindful of the present moment.

It is imperative to decelerate. You have a solitary existence to traverse, so refrain from hasting through it, and abstain from relying on anything that instigates a sense of urgency. Remain calm and decelerate.

Engaging in a period of tranquil contemplation and deliberate deep breathing lasting for a duration of 10 minutes. Recite the affirmation: "Adopt a decelerated pace." Do not rush. Find delight in the current moment."

Please document and share this experience by utilizing the hashtag #30DaysCount.

Day 5

Exercise:

Observe your body. Take note of the sensations, movements, and responses. Further guidance is elucidated in the succeeding sections.

If you are currently undergoing feelings of anxiety, I advise you to engage in the act of mindful observation. Take note of the subtle shifts in your bodily movements, sounds, sensations, and breath patterns that arise during this aforementioned experience. Do your eyes widen? How do you breathe? Do you possess a propensity for swift or gradual movement? What is the tonal quality of your voice? How is your posture? Do you sweat? Make an effort to carefully observe every aspect of your body while experiencing anxiety. Keep in mind the impact of anxiety on your physical well-being.

If you are currently not encountering anxiety, we invite you to proceed with the practice of maintaining a period of 10 minutes of silence and engaged breathing. However, we encourage you to establish a connection with your physical being. A beneficial approach to accomplish this objective would involve physically making contact with each body part, enunciating its respective name, and subsequently maintaining contact for a brief period to discern its texture and warmth. Initiate with your cranium: gently rest your hand upon your head and vocally acknowledge, "I am making contact with my cranium." Proceed systematically to address your upper extremities consisting of the shoulders and arms, followed by your midsection, lower limbs encompassing the stomach, legs, knees, and finally concluding with acknowledgement of your feet. Direct your attention to individual body parts sequentially. Please articulate the appellation of the object and proceed to provide a thorough description of the tactile experience you are presently encountering. Please proceed at the slowest pace feasible; refrain from hastening the observation.

Similar to various detrimental affections, anxiety possesses the ability to deceive one into perceiving that it has dominion over their physical being, to the extent of convincing them that they are merely a puppet under its control. Reclaim ownership of your physical being by cultivating mindfulness through the act of diligent observation. Engaging in intentional observation of your physical state during instances of anxiety provides an excellent opportunity to uncover the fallacy of anxious thoughts.

The Value of Social Interaction

An effective approach to comprehending the term "outgoing" is to linguistically dissect it into two distinct components: "out" and "going." This can be interpreted literally, such as engaging in regular outings from one's place of residence. This rationale is justified since individuals with less sociable or extroverted tendencies often devote significant periods of time in seclusion within their residences or indoor settings due to their inherent shyness. Possessing an extroverted demeanor entails openly manifesting or unveiling one's personality rather than concealing it. Put simply, by fully embodying your true self.

It proves advantageous to be a member of a close-knit community wherein individuals engage in social interactions and provide assistance to one another. Coping with life's pressures singlehandedly can prove challenging; acquiring the ability to collaborate with others can significantly enhance the quality of your life. As commonly stated, there is power in collective unity. It is advantageous to understand that participation in a collective can assist an individual in combating external challenges. However, it is particularly intriguing to ascertain that profound social acceptance can also promote the mastery of internal obstacles, such as physical well-being concerns. Many individuals tend to overlook the importance of being in the presence of others. However, embracing a greater degree of sociability brings forth numerous benefits.

"Consider the ensuing benefits of fostering increased sociability:

1. Practical Benefits

Individuals who exhibit timidness or possess introverted tendencies often find themselves susceptible to feelings of isolation. This may alternatively indicate that the individual in question is susceptible to developing depression, given that loneliness frequently precedes the onset of depressive symptoms. However, it must be noted that loneliness does not necessarily indicate depression; it can arise due to various other factors too.

Nevertheless, should individuals actively engage in social interactions with their loved ones, acquaintances, or participate in community events more frequently, they may experience a decrease in feelings of loneliness. Ensuring the presence of social support remains crucial in mitigating feelings of isolation. By possessing a robust network of assistance, one will enhance their efficacy and vitality, ultimately attaining a definitive sense of purpose in their existence.

2. Health Benefits

People who are in close proximity to others have a decreased likelihood of experiencing health concerns. Based on the findings of researchers, an individual experiencing isolation exhibits a diminished immune system, affecting their ability to effectively uphold and restore the bodily processes essential for optimal physiological functioning. Through engaging in social interactions, individuals can cultivate a heightened immune response, thereby enhancing their ability to combat various infections.

Additionally, additional research has demonstrated that social connections and effective communication abilities can decrease the likelihood of mortality. For example, factors such as enhanced social interactions with family members and friends can greatly expedite the recuperation process for individuals facing medical ailments like heart disease or post-surgical patients.

3. Stress Reducer

The presence of familiar individuals, such as beloved friends and cherished family members, can effectively contribute to alleviating stress. Allocating one's time to be in the company of individuals who hold significant importance in their life can provide respite from the burdensome concerns that occupy their mind. Therefore, engaging in social activities and enjoying oneself serves as a means of alleviating physiological and psychological stress. Indulging in solitary laughter serves as an effective means of alleviating stress and negative emotions, and when combined with cultivating robust interpersonal connections, one can acquire the necessary support system to effectively confront any stressors encountered in life.

4. Career Benefits

Possessing proficient social skills can have a profound influence on your professional endeavors. In contemporary society, the acquisition of effective social and communication skills significantly contributes to job retention. In contemporary times, an effective strategy for differentiating oneself is to cultivate a greater degree of likability. In order to accomplish this, it is imperative to possess the knowledge and skills required to establish efficacious and mutually beneficial relationships within the professional setting. Nobody has the ability to enhance your likability more than you do. Proficiency in interpersonal communication enables individuals to establish a deeper understanding of others on an intimate level.

It is evident that cultivating a more extroverted demeanor and honing one's communication prowess can yield considerably greater benefits in one's life beyond current awareness. By implementing adjustments in this particular sphere of your existence, you have the opportunity to cultivate new social connections, forge romantic relationships, foster professional networks, and establish a prosperous vocation, among other notable benefits. Therefore, cease any hesitations and wholeheartedly embrace the opportunities that life presents!

Conduct a thorough exploration of a scenario until its conclusion

The final technique for managing anxiety that you will acquire is to fully enact a given scenario until its conclusion. In this scenario, you are encouraged to contemplate and deliberate upon your apprehensions, and grant yourself the opportunity to thoroughly contemplate the potential outcomes of that specific circumstance. As an instance, let us consider the possibility that you harbor apprehension regarding potential job loss when you resume work tomorrow after being absent due to illness for an extensive duration of one week. Your heightened state of anxiety is preventing you from achieving restful sleep, despite your awareness of the necessity for slumber.

In this instance, it is advisable to halt your actions, deliberate upon the fear at hand, and subsequently envision the anticipated outcome of the situation. If you harbor concerns about potential termination upon your arrival, envision the plausible outcomes you anticipate. It is possible that you envision a scenario in which you make an arrival and your supervisor approaches you. Instead of informing you that a private conversation is necessary, your superior inquires about your well-being and expresses that your presence was missed. He refrains from mentioning your illness due to his admirable managerial skills and empathetic understanding that individuals may occasionally experience health setbacks.

Due to the portrayal of the realistic outcome, you possess the ability to juxtapose it with the hypothetical worst-case circumstance that you might have concurrently constructed for that specific scenario. You have the capability to observe both situations and comprehend that you will remain unharmed. You are aware that termination of employment is a potential outcome, however, it is consistently a possibility. At any given employment, one must acknowledge the potentiality of being terminated, irrespective of the circumstances. Subsequently, you can commence to unwind and assure yourself that circumstances will improve, thereby facilitating your eventual slumber and attainment of the necessary rest.

Approaches for Enhancing Quality of Life

Now, you will be guided through a series of steps aimed at enhancing the quality of your life. The following are alternative methods that can prove advantageous to individuals, notwithstanding their primary focus may not exclusively center on anxiety alleviation. These methods have the potential to enhance one's overall satisfaction and meaning in life. While progressing through this procedure and perusing the aforementioned four distinct activities, consider envisioning the conceivable application of any of these prospects to your personal existence, thereby facilitating the realization of the desired trajectory of your life. It is possible to perceive that there exist various methodologies by which one could introduce greater positivity into their life, thereby potentially reducing their anxiety levels.

Goal Setting

The initial skill being presented to you pertains to the establishment of appropriate objectives. Objectives are commonly established by individuals, yet frequently they are ill-considered, resulting in subsequent failure and subsequent relinquishment with little further contemplation. Nonetheless, this can be attributed predominantly to the absence of properly defined objectives. By attaining proficiency in establishing effective goals, one enhances their likelihood of achieving success.

When establishing objectives, it is imperative to consider certain factors that should never serve as the focus of a goal: avoiding specific outcomes, being based solely on one's emotional state, or involving desires to revisit the past. Each of these three subjects to pursue for your goal will inevitably lead to failure and must be strictly avoided.

12. The Influence of Humor

For an extensive period, medical practitioners have maintained the belief that individuals' mental dispositions can significantly impact the duration and overall outcome of their recovery from an illness.

The manifestation of mirth and the expression of amusement are catalysts for beneficial physiological transformations within the human organism. It enhances your vitality, mitigates discomfort, all the while shielding you from the deleterious impacts of stress and anxiety. Essentially, the act of engaging in hearty laughter and humor has the effect of inducing a deep sense of relaxation and alleviating physical tension and stress, resulting in the subsequent relaxation of muscles for a duration of approximately 45 minutes. In addition to the aforementioned advantages, the following benefits accrue to you:

Enhancement of the immune system: Laughter not only reduces the presence of stress hormones but also elevates the production of immune cells and antibodies that combat infections. This ultimately aids in the development of heightened immunity against illnesses.

Stimulation of positive neurochemicals: Engaging in laughter can stimulate the release of endorphins, which are the body's inherent hormones associated with feelings of well-being. With elevated levels of endorphins in the body, individuals are apt to experience an enhancement in their overall state of well-being. Furthermore, it will become evident that frequent laughter results in significant alleviation of pain.

Safeguarding your cardiovascular health - The act of laughing enhances vascular function and promotes blood circulation, thereby providing a defense against potential heart ailments such as heart attacks and other cardiovascular disorders.

14. Addressing Distorted Thinking Patterns and Surrendering Control

One may not fully comprehend the extent to which thoughts can fuel anxiety. Nonetheless, it is a fact that these thoughts may serve as the primary cause of your persistent anxiety. Therefore, should your thoughts induce anxiety, it becomes imperative to diligently observe and manage them in order to achieve true relief from anxiety. What are a few of the thought patterns that might contribute to your experience of anxiety?

To begin with, an aspect worthy of consideration is the prominent cognitive tendency that potentially contributes to your anxiety, which involves employing definitive language and engaging in absolutist thinking. In this particular instance, the thoughts and conversations you engage in consist of words such as always, no one, never, should, must, everyone, and other analogous expressions. Regrettably, these thoughts exhibit inflexibility and impose an excessive burden upon you, rendering the situation appear and feel hopeless. Consequently, your propensity for heightened anxiety is greatly increased. Merely refraining from the utilization of such language can serve as an initial stride in combating anxiety.

An alternative perspective involves harboring impractical feelings of insecurity regarding various situations. As an illustration, individuals who possess a proclivity for inquiring "what if" in nearly every circumstance may anticipate experiencing numerous occurrences of unease. The positive information is that you have the capacity to effectively modify these ingrained thought patterns. May I inquire about the methodology to accomplish the aforementioned task? Consider conceptualizing your thoughts as a mechanism resembling a wheel. Rotating this wheel will generate sparks. Think of these sparks as the anxious thoughts of "what if" such as "what if he/she hurts me, what if they laugh at me, what if I have an accident, what if he/she cheats on me" etc. Ceasing the rotation of said wheel will directly result in the cessation of your anxiety as well. In summary, you possess complete authority over the timing and duration for which you manipulate this wheel.

Make an effort to recognize all the distorted cognitive patterns that you possess, and subsequently contemplate the extent of distress these thoughts may evoke within you. Once the thoughts have been identified, they can subsequently be substituted with more equitable alternatives. Indeed, it is imperative to acknowledge that attaining freedom from anxiety does not manifest instantaneously. However, through consistent dedication and repetition, one can gradually observe a shift in thought patterns, resulting in a more automated mental process that no longer fixates on the previously ingrained notions. You even find it peculiar that you once possessed such thought patterns! However, when faced with circumstances beyond your jurisdiction, it is imperative to cultivate an attitude of acceptance and adapt to it in order to persevere. This holds particularly true due to the fact that attempting to exert control over something that is outside of one's sphere of influence inevitably induces physiological and psychological strain, thereby intensifying feelings of anxiety.

Magical Pathways to Joy

Given the myriad of challenges we encounter on a daily basis, be it within academic pursuits or professional endeavors, the attainment of happiness may prove to be an arduous undertaking. The global landscape is becoming progressively more challenging and intricate The regular patterns we engage in on a daily basis can occasionally prove detrimental to our mental and physical well-being.

However, it is fortunate to note that regardless of the severity of one's experience, there remains an opportunity for the presence of joy. You have the ability to experience happiness should you choose to do so. Stress is merely a consequence of your appraisal. If one perceives an event to be stressful, it can be asserted that it is indeed a source of stress.

The human mind is a significant factor in shaping one's perception of the external environment. If you allow yourself to be consumed by negative thoughts, you will be unable to fully appreciate the beauty that surrounds you. Therefore, a means of attaining enduring happiness lies in comprehending that stress arises from a flawed cognitive assessment.

Once you alter your perception of your experience, you will attain a state of cognitive alignment conducive to promoting healthy thinking patterns. The concept of happiness may vary among individuals. The richness in our array of perspectives and emotions contributes to our distinct interpretations of happiness. For generations, an array of scholars including philosophers, theologians, and psychologists have endeavored to delineate and characterize this complex emotional phenomenon. Consequently, this construct acquires various interpretations.

Nevertheless, certain interpretations are comparatively more apparent than their counterparts. The prevailing interpretation posits that happiness is a cognitive state of overall wellness encompassing positive emotions. Individuals who possess a favorable assessment of their present life circumstances generally experience a sense of happiness.

However, the true inquiry lies not in the manner in which we determine happiness, but rather in how we attain a state of genuine happiness. What is the manner in which individuals of our contemporary era cultivate a positive self-image? In the realm of animosity, prejudice, and scrutiny, the pursuit of happiness becomes a challenging endeavor. It assumes the status of a prized asset that the majority of individuals are unable to procure.

Fortunately, happiness is free. This is the truth. We have made a deliberate choice to overlook or disregard this particular aspect of reality. We embrace the notion that life is inherently challenging and replete with hardships. However, in reality, this is not the case. Outlined below are the fundamental measures to attain happiness in one's life.

1. Extend well wishes to others

Do you currently experience any particular physical affliction? Are you burdened by financial indebtedness? Alternatively, are you encountering difficulties within your present relationship? Perhaps you are under the impression that your current experiences are predominantly unfavorable. Hence, it is evident that you harbor feelings of jealousy towards others. However, your interpretation is incorrect. Indeed, you are perfectly timed to extend your best wishes to them. Desiring the utmost well-being for others can engender personal happiness. The sensation of delight is predominantly derived from the external realm. It entails establishing and fostering interpersonal connections while displaying genuine care and consideration for others. If one experiences a sense of contentment at the accomplishments of others, they may inadvertently be experiencing internal gratification. That is the path to true happiness.

2. Imagine yourself having already accomplished the goals you aspire to achieve.

What is your ultimate objective? Can it be regarded as an exquisite automobile, a fruitful and harmonious companionship, an educational attainment from a reputable institution of higher learning, or a substantial accomplishment in terms of finances? The prevailing notion among individuals is that achieving success proves to be quite arduous. Frequently, individuals fail to acknowledge their inherent potential for attaining both happiness and success. To achieve success in life, it is imperative to adopt the persona of a successful individual. It may appear frivolous, however, it is indeed factual. Maintain a clear and unwavering focus on your goal. By this, I am referring to the notion that if you aspire to possess an opulent automobile, it is imperative to cultivate a regular practice of consistently dwelling upon the idea of owning said vehicle. Envision yourself operating the vehicle. This procedure facilitates the development of self-awareness regarding one's genuine capabilities. Many individuals tend to overlook the fact that their mind, being the most formidable tool at their disposal, holds tremendous power. Whatever ideas the intellect envisions, they shall manifest into actuality.

3. Embrace the aesthetic allure of all aspects.

Frequently, our attention is directed towards unfavorable occurrences or aspects in our life. Consequently, we often fail to perceive the positive aspects in our surroundings. It is imperative to bear in mind that in every adverse circumstance, there exists a corresponding favorable aspect. In order to attain happiness, it is advisable to direct your attention towards constructive and affirmative elements. Discover something that evokes a sense of pure delight within you. Does it happen to be a musical composition? A painting? A poem or novel? Engage in a thorough exploration of your surroundings to recognize and value the elements that bring you joy and satisfaction.

4. Foster positive interpersonal connections with others.

There exist several factors that have the potential to evoke feelings of happiness in an individual. Finance is amongst the factors under consideration. However, it should be noted that monetary prosperity does not exclusively determine one's level of contentment. Several scholarly investigations on happiness have revealed that a key determinant of our overall happiness is a positive and fulfilling interpersonal connection. Naturally, a relationship entails establishing a strong rapport with individuals. It could pertain to a close interpersonal connection, such as a romantic partner or familial bond. Indeed, the prosperity of an entire nation is intricately linked to the strength of its social connections, rather than solely relying on a strong economy.

5. Maintain positive thoughts

Regardless of your actions, strive to uphold a state of positive energy coursing through your being. By this, I am implying that you must exercise caution and awareness regarding your thoughts. Avoid negative thinking. It poisons your well-being. As uncertainty about one's own abilities arises, it inevitably becomes an impediment to the achievement of the intended objective. Individuals with a tendency towards negativity are unlikely to attain their desired objectives. Why? Due to their perception of their own inability. Once you believe that you are incapable, you will inevitably fail to achieve your objective. It is essential to bear in mind that your thoughts possess the potential to shape your reality.

6. Discover inner peace.

Joy springs forth from the discovery of one's own existence being subjected to equitable assessment. Release yourself from the grasp of those adverse encounters. The events of yesterday have minimal impact on your current circumstances. Acquire the skill of abstaining from matters beyond your control. And remain hopeful. Commence the creation of your promising future. If you persist in harboring pessimistic thoughts, you will inevitably find yourself immersed in feelings of sorrow. Therefore, make every effort to attain serenity in spite of your present circumstances.

7. Maximize your potential

The majority of individuals tend to lose sight of their true identity. They hold the belief that they are incapable of accomplishing anything. However, the reality remains that they possess a greater level of competence than they perceive. Their self-proclaimed weakness, namely their negative thoughts, presents the sole obstacle to their achievement of success. Furthermore, they fail to recognize the magnitude of their latent abilities. To attain a life of contentment, one must actively capitalize on one's inherent capabilities. Establish objectives today and engage in their pursuit.

8. Choose to cultivate a positive disposition.

The most indispensable approach to attaining happiness is to make a deliberate choice to pursue it. If one harbors deep-seated feelings of animosity and jealousy while yearning for personal happiness, attaining such happiness will remain elusive. To experience delight, it is imperative to liberate oneself from negative emotions. It requires a great deal of bravery to accomplish such a task. It entails not merely donning a smile on a daily basis, but rather, embodying a consistently optimistic emotional disposition.

9. Never blame

In instances of failure or errors in judgment, refrain from assigning blame to any individual or external factor. Embrace the experience of failure and derive valuable lessons from it. Seek means of effectively addressing the issue at hand. Direct your attention towards the opportunities within your control rather than dwelling on limitations. Accusing others is an unproductive allocation of one's time and effort. Be wise enough.

10. Provide what is essential.

Most people have goals. However, the issue at hand pertains to the disparity between the tasks assigned and the actual requirements to accomplish said goals. Greater aspirations require increased effort and diligence. Insufficient alignment between your objective and the exertion of your endeavor will impede your attainment of success. It is imperative that you exert the requisite level of effort.

11. Engage in moments of quiet contemplation

The optimal location for discovering happiness lies in moments of tranquility. Allocate some time to disconnect yourself from the bustling world. Make reflections of yourself. Visualize all the positive experiences that have transpired throughout your existence. What are those? And what are your aspirations for the future? Stillness facilitates a profound connection with the intangible energies present in one's surroundings. Devote time to attain true happiness.

12. Please exercise vigilance in maintaining your physical well-being.

The interdependence of mental health and physical health cannot be disregarded. An unbalanced psyche may have adverse effects on the physical well-being. Furthermore, it should be noted that ailing physical health can also have an impact on one's mental well-being. According to this doctrine, authentic happiness cannot be attained in the presence of physical ailments. Numerous studies have demonstrated a correlation between physical ailments in adults and their diminished psychological well-being. The attribute that experiences the greatest impact is the state of one's psychological well-being.

It is highly advisable to prioritize the maintenance of one's physical well-being. Refrain from consuming unhealthy food items, such as fast food, carbonated beverages, and the like. Engage in daily physical activity and establish a consistent sleep routine at an early hour. Remaining awake into the late hours of the night will have detrimental ramifications on both your physical and mental well-being.

13. Avoid overthinking

In order to attain a state of contentment, it is imperative to liberate one's mind from excessive rumination. Overthinking occurs when excessive concern is directed towards forthcoming events. Your evaluation of this uncertain matter appears to be overly exaggerated. It will not yield any beneficial outcomes.

To attain happiness, one must engage in a reasoned assessment. Refrain from exerting self-imposed pressure to assume responsibility for a task in which you lack the necessary aptitude. Envision a promising and exhilarating future in your mind's eye. Release your anxieties and allow the events of tomorrow to happen without interference. By acknowledging and embracing your limitations, you will be able to liberate your mind from excessive rumination.

14. Compose a catalog of your minor accomplishments.

Whether you choose to acknowledge it or not, you are consistently accomplishing remarkable feats on a daily basis. However, this fact frequently eludes the majority. They only perceive frustrations and defeat. To attain happiness, it is imperative to recognize and value the incremental achievements and advancements experienced on a daily basis.

One can achieve this by creating a comprehensive inventory. Develop the practice of documenting your minor accomplishments. This experience will not only contribute to your happiness, but also serve as a reminder of the significant achievements you have already attained. It is important to bear in mind that the sole path towards achieving your objective is through consistently performing small actions on a daily basis. And these incremental actions will culminate in a significant triumph.

15. Smile

It is truly remarkable to discover that scientific research has confirmed the beneficial effects of a mere smile. The act of smiling leads to an increase in serotonin levels within the brain. Serotonin is a neuromodulator or a neurochemical in the central nervous system that enhances emotional well-being. On a daily basis, seek justification for engaging in the task. Indulge in the pleasure of watching a beloved comedy film or seek the company of someone who has a knack for eliciting laughter. This straightforward gesture is adequate to attain a state of contentment.

16. Be grateful

For a significant duration, both average individuals and scholars have been actively searching for the optimal path to attaining a state of contentment. Numerous studies indicate that attaining happiness is inherently cost-free. Indeed, a research study revealed that happiness stems from expressing gratitude for one's minor accomplishments.

Individuals who compile a record of elements for which they experience gratitude tend to exhibit greater levels of happiness compared to their counterparts who refrain from engaging in this practice. The favorable aspect is that on a daily basis, a multitude of positive occurrences come your way. The sole issue lies in the fact that you made a conscious decision to overlook them. One typically observes predominantly adverse occurrences. In order to cultivate genuine happiness, it is advisable to develop an inclination towards acknowledging the small blessings and joys that grace your existence.

17. Immerse yourself in the company of individuals who exude happiness.

Stress is contagious. To attain happiness, it is advisable to steer clear of individuals who exhibit pessimistic tendencies. They can't help you. On the contrary, seek out individuals who possess a positive demeanor capable of enlivening your daily experiences. They not only bring about happiness, but also serve as a source of motivation to propel one forward.

18. Engage in interaction with your domestic animals.

Owning a pet can enhance one's emotional well-being. Numerous studies have substantiated the notion that individuals who keep pets experience a notably higher level of happiness compared to those who do not possess companion animals. Individuals who possess an affinity for animals tend to experience greater levels of subjective well-being.

19. It is advisable to abstain from watching the news.

If one engages with television broadcasts and various forms of media in order to stay informed, it becomes evident that the likelihood of encountering positive news is comparatively lower than that of encountering negative news. Put simply, positive news is rarely found within the media. Unfortunately, the downside is that adverse news possesses the capability to proliferate like a contagion.

It shall obscure your cognition, ultimately leading to a pessimistic outlook on the world.

If one desires genuine happiness, it would be advisable to disengage from television and refrain from exposure to pessimistic news. Rather, take the time to express gratitude for all the positive occurrences that transpired throughout the entirety of the day. This will enhance your comfort and uplift your happiness.

20. Forgive and forget

We are all travellers. As we proceed on our journey, we encounter individuals who bring us joy and/or evoke vexation. Indeed, in more severe instances, individuals would scorn or degrade us. Regardless of the outcome, refrain from harboring feelings of anger and seeking retribution. It is most advisable to extend forgiveness and let go of past grievances. Disregard all individuals who have caused you pain. Focus on your goals. Remain unconcerned about the opinions that others may hold regarding you. As a result, you will experience an increase in happiness.

Being able to read people

Gaining the ability to effectively comprehend individuals is a skill that proves indispensable in various circumstances, and fortunately, its acquisition does not have to be arduous. By following a concise set of instructions, one can initiate comprehension of the thoughts manifesting within the minds of individuals, thereby enabling the interpretation of their behavioral patterns and emotional states. One's actions and emotions will inevitably be shaped by the influence of others, highlighting the importance of attaining the skill to interpret and comprehend the expressions of others. Fortunately, you have the opportunity to adhere to this comprehensive manual: "

Firstly, it is imperative to ascertain the individual's personality type.

In order to gain insights into the individuals in your environment, it is imperative to commence by ascertaining the personality trait classification of the individual in question. There exists a multitude of methods to accomplish this task, however, the most effortless approach entails discerning a handful of uncomplicated factors that manifest while observing an individual. You will be observing their navigation abilities as well as their responses. Upon examination, one will gain insights into the nature of the individuals with whom they come into contact.

Initially, contemplate the distinction between sensing and intuitiveness. This represents the initial distinction you are about to examine. Certain individuals have a tendency to align themselves by relying on their senses. They actively seek evidential and supportive information, which ultimately cultivates a more intuitive nature. Such individuals prioritize their current emotions and focus on their internal sensations. It is essential to ensure one pays heed to this matter. As one observes an individual's personality traits and closely monitors their choices and behavior in their interactions with the world, novel patterns begin to emerge. Gaining insight into their mental processes and cognitive patterns is crucial in delineating their behaviors. This initial stage will afford you with the opportunity to gain such valuable insight.

Subsequently, one must contemplate whether their response to the world is primarily driven by cognitive processes or emotional manifestations. Are they prioritizing the fulfillment of their emotions? Is the pursuit underway for them to experience a sense of contentment? Are they actively seeking methods to deliberate upon their respective circumstances? Intellectual individuals are often motivated primarily by their own faculty of reason and logic, deliberately engaging with the world by adhering to predetermined principles and guidelines. They are more inclined to adhere to those rules. Individuals with a heightened sense of emotion, conversely, are motivated by their affective experiences. They take into account both values and the specific circumstances, rather than attempting to impose them in a way that aligns artificially with my natural disposition.

Once you embark upon this line of reasoning, you can subsequently evaluate the temperament of the individual with whom you are conversing, specifically determining whether they lean towards introversion or extroversion. Introverted individuals are characterized by their inclination to be inwardly focused, as they tend to direct their attention towards their own thoughts and emotions, resulting in a quieter demeanor. Their primary focus lies in self-contemplation and self-conduct, and their excessive exposure to social settings often leaves them feeling emotionally depleted. In group settings, they tend to adopt a demeanor of quiet observation, appearing somewhat overwhelmed when thrust into the spotlight.

In stark contrast, extroverts generally derive immense pleasure from occupying the spotlight. They derive immense pleasure from social interactions, experiencing utmost satisfaction when they engage effectively with fellow individuals. They demonstrate a propensity for action over introspection, and typically exhibit a greater degree of comfort in social environments.

Step 2: Get the base reading of their body language

Subsequently, once you have established an initial understanding of the individual you intend to analyze, you can proceed to concentrate on acquiring an initial understanding. Prior to commencing, it is imperative to ascertain the thoughts and intentions of individuals involved, ensuring that one can discern the presence or absence of typical behavior. Consider this: an introverted individual is unlikely to display excessive enthusiasm by raising their hands aimlessly, while an extroverted individual is unlikely to avoid eye contact during a conversation. Gaining comprehension of this concept will facilitate your ability to analyze the fundamental non-verbal cues, thereby enabling you to determine its authenticity and spontaneity.

Acquiring a preliminary understanding of another individual's body language assumes paramount significance prior to commencing the process of interpretation. This comprehensive resource will provide you with a fundamental framework for comprehending the underlying thought processes and perspectives of the individual in question. Consider this scenario: while operating your vehicle, you become aware that your fuel efficiency is at an average of 20 miles per gallon. What would be your reaction to this? Do you perceive this to be advantageous or disadvantageous? The response solely relies on the base MPG that you anticipate. A truck achieving a fuel efficiency of 20 miles per gallon may be considered relatively satisfactory, as a significant number of trucks have earned a reputation for being highly fuel-consuming. In contrast, a recently acquired Prius that achieves a fuel efficiency of merely 20 miles per gallon suggests a severe underlying issue, as the mileage is nearly halved compared to the expected performance. This consideration holds significant importance: It is imperative to possess not only the ability to comprehend the situation, but also the requisite contextual understanding. One must possess the capability to discern the true nature of a situation, ascertaining its merit or detriment by means of comparison against its inherent state.

Regarding nonverbal communication, this entails examining inherent conditions. To effectively understand someone's thoughts and emotions during a conversation, it is crucial to observe their foundational non-verbal cues prior to initiating the interaction. This task is commonly accomplished by observing the individual's natural interactions in an unpressured environment, or engaging in a preliminary conversation with a third party as a preparatory step towards understanding their behavior. During the course of that introductory dialogue, ensure that you diligently observe their manner of interaction with you. How are they conducting themselves? What activities are they engaging in? Observe their comportment and ascertain their preferred posture.

Step 3: Observe incongruities in their nonverbal cues

Furthermore, it is important to take into account the possibility of identifying any inconsistencies. This phenomenon occurs during the current interaction, as one observes the actions and behaviors involved in the engagement, leading to the identification and interpretation of the disparities. Upon observing those, one will be able to discern the various patterns of conduct. This is the juncture at which their nonverbal cues will start to convey all the information that you require. During your interaction, you will have the opportunity to observe how the individual is actively participating. Are they demonstrating an unusual display of shyness? Are they frequently averting their gaze? Are they exhibiting flirtatious behavior towards you? Commence the search for indications. Commence observing their behavior. Please take note of any inconsistencies with the initial baseline body language that you have determined and ensure that you allocate adequate time and effort to observe it more attentively.

Step 4: Discern the groups of behaviors

Subsequently, it is imperative to commence the development of coherent groups of behaviors. This is the juncture at which one should begin contemplating the contextual implications of the observed body language. Do they avert their gaze due to fear or as a result of deception? It may be necessary for you to observe alternative nonverbal cues in order to gain a comprehensive understanding of their current state. By gaining an understanding of those distinct sets of behaviors, you can consequently develop an understanding of your own actions and the manner in which they are carried out. You will gain a comprehensive comprehension of the interplay and synergy between all elements involved.

For instance, let us consider the scenario of a woman whose gaze is directed towards the ground. It is possible that she is experiencing nerves, timidity, or a general sense of unease. She may also experience feelings of embarrassment. You should also direct your attention to all other aspects in conjunction with it. It is imperative that you seek out alternative indications in order to discern the distinction. An individual displaying signs of nervousness may exhibit behaviors such as crossing their arms and shifting in an attempt to self-soothe. Similarly, someone who is experiencing embarrassment may demonstrate involuntary blushing and difficulties in speaking fluently. It is imperative to consider alternative indicators in order to comprehend the current situation.

In the context of discerning patterns of conduct, it is imperative to carefully observe the recurring manifestation of identical behaviors. You are seeking indications of recurring patterns in these behaviors, thereby discerning their consistency rather than dismissing them as isolated occurrences. Taking into account this aspect and being mindful of it will aid you in guaranteeing that you can obtain the most accurate reading feasible.

Step 5: Analyzing the clusters of behavioral patterns

Ultimately, the concluding phase in this entire process entails ensuring a thorough analysis is conducted. Observe the actions and emotions, and subsequently analyze the underlying reasons for their manifestation. Kindly direct your attention to the manner in which individuals often actively participate. Take into account the circumstances surrounding their current situation. Is their response rational and logical? Do they appear to be disproportionate? All of these factors will assist you in determining the appropriate course of action and adopting the proper response to the behaviors to which you are exposed. The more expediently you acquire the skill of comprehending those behaviors, the more promptly you can proceed to analyze and interpret them.

The Knowledge Acquired in Cognitive Behavioral Therapy

Initially, you will acquire the ability to modify your thought process and subsequent behavior. Please be reminded that this therapeutic approach derives from cognitive foundations and focuses on behavioral modification. It is imperative due to the consistent interconnectedness of thoughts, feelings, and behavior at any given moment. Every individual aspect contributes to the others, perpetuating the cycle until you address each or all of them.

Returning to our illustration concerning the apprehension of those who possess greater physical strength – envision a scenario in which you encounter an individual who consistently requests something from you prior to entering your residential area. The level of anticipation is excessively heightened as you contemplate your course of action. Due to his persistent pursuit of his demands, it is imperative that you either opt for an alternative course, albeit a longer one, or acquiesce to his desires.

Based on an analysis of the interconnection diagram, the following depiction illustrates the arrangement:

MEETING THE BULLY

Nevertheless, if one contemplates an approach to resolve the situation with the prominent acquaintance, he may be amenable to considering a solution that aligns with his interests, or employing a strategy that ensures minimal interference on his part. When communicating, please consider using lawful methods rather than engaging in foolish actions. Now, let us return to our established pattern. "It will have a different appearance, similar to this:

MEETING THE BULLY

Taking into consideration the aforementioned factors, individuals may opt to utilize the subsequent strategies in order to effectively address the issue of the bully:

Alternative 1: Altered Behavioral Mode

Initially, by circumventing the circumstances and adopting an approach that diminishes the strength of the friend, there will be the provision of pertinent information to him as well as the implementation of a strategy to assuage the situation from the perspective of the victim. Subsequently, it will become apparent in one's cognition that we are all members of the human race, and our behavior may vary between rational and irrational, contingent upon the prevailing circumstances. In this manner, individuals are afforded the opportunity to become acquainted with one another prior to engaging in a conversation that will alleviate any subsequent unease.

Although movies are essentially visual narratives, we can glean this moral lesson from the protagonists' journey as they successfully navigate the challenges presented before them.

Alternative 2: Adjusting the Cognitive Perspective

Additionally, one can aptly question the rationale underpinning the intimidation experienced due to the aggressor. It will be recalled later that the primary motivation behind this approach is to prevent oneself from being placed in a situation wherein one would be obliged to fulfill his requests. In that manner, you will possess the knowledge that you are not obliged to provide them with what they require if it does not align with your authorized access document.

We are motivated by apprehension due to our perception of the necessity to submit in the event of encountering the individual. Subsequently, one may experience a sense of unease and become unable to perceive the complete panorama. Given your fear, it is conceivable to consistently contemplate the potential detriment that could arise, rather than focusing on actions that will prompt individuals to retreat and cease bothering you. When an individual possesses a state of mental equilibrium, they are able to perceive things and situations through a lucid lens, thereby equipping the mind with the requisite resources to confront apprehension.

An Exposition on the Biological Mechanisms Underlying Stress

As demonstrated in the preceding chapter, stress and anxiety present a significant peril to both our physical and psychological well-being, inciting numerous symptoms that may go unnoticed as being attributable to stress-induced factors. However, what is the root cause of this occurrence? What is the physiological response occurring within our bodies during instances of stress? What is the underlying cause for our distress and impairment in performing daily tasks at a satisfactory level?

An interdependence exists between the mind and body, as it has been determined.

It is likely apparent to you that during periods of emotional distress, one may observe the exacerbation of underlying health concerns, such as the emergence of skin issues or insomnia, as prime examples. One observes that stress, in essence, manifests as a bodily and intellectual reaction to a circumstance which one perceives as beyond their ability to effectively handle, whether that perception is conscious or unconscious. If one holds the conviction that the matter warrants concern, then indeed, apprehension shall ensue, even if one remains unaware of its manifestation.

When an individual encounters stress, their physiological response is initiated. But what exactly happens? Let's take a look.

Your Stress Response

Consider this scenario: as you traverse the highway, your attention is drawn to the presence of an upturned lorry obstructing the entirety of the road. It will prove exceedingly challenging to elude, and your entire physique readies itself for the nearly inescapable encounter.

This crisis triggers a cascade of hormonal reactions that effectively prepares your body to confront the forthcoming challenges. This is achieved through the release of the stress hormones cortisol, adrenaline, and norepinephrine, which facilitate your ability to confront and respond to the current circumstances. These hormones facilitate enhanced circulation and oxygen supply to critical areas such as the head and muscles, inevitably diverting resources from other bodily regions to optimize the likelihood of survival. Furthermore, they elevate your blood sugar levels with the purpose of adequately nourishing the muscles, in order to facilitate the response of either combat or escape.

A Wasted Response

The successive chain of responses has facilitated our long-standing survival spanning millennia. The hardship lies in the fact that although this approach proved to be ideal for ancestral humans seeking shelter from predators, its efficacy in the present era is somewhat diminished.

The reaction is not solely incited by physical stimuli that affect our well-being, but also by a growing array of psychological factors. Your physique interprets challenging circumstances such as examinations, enduring traffic, conflicts with loved ones, demanding routines, and insufficient sleep as potential dangers, thus inciting identical stress responses. This is particularly true if you are already experiencing feelings of vulnerability and being overwhelmed by your current life circumstances.

The issue lies in the fact that this particular stress response does not become depleted. There is no necessity for you to escape or engage in combat. Consequently, you are compelled to endure the challenges of managing elevated blood sugar levels, the consequential deprivation of vital blood and oxygen to your organs, ultimately resulting in a sensation akin to a tightly wound coil. Furthermore, these circumstances may give rise to a multitude of health issues, including but not limited to elevated blood pressure, the onset of Alzheimer's disease, cardiovascular complications, disruptions in hormonal equilibrium, depressive disorders, excessive weight gain, and impairments in sexual functionality.

Stress and anxiety represent our finely tuned physiological reactions to peril, yet unharnessed.

Undoubtedly, a certain level of stress is to be expected and can yield advantageous outcomes. In what other manner might we acquire the impetus to rise at dawn and confront the forthcoming day? What compels us to pursue our aspirations, if not for the presence of a certain degree of stress?

However, the issue at hand pertains to the elevated levels of stress that we are currently encountering. We lack the necessary resources to effectively deal with this situation, hence it is unsurprising that we experience such emotions.

It is imperative to assume command.

Certainly, it should be acknowledged that the stressful circumstances we have examined in this do not solely account for stress and anxiety. It is imperative to recognize that a multitude of other factors exist, which possess the potential to contribute to difficulties or exacerbate preexisting ones. Could you kindly clarify the nature of these entities and propose possible courses of action? It is now imperative to ascertain.

Fourth Step: Strategies to Mitigate Anxiety in the Subsequent Periods

We have examined measures to address transient anxiety. This segment will primarily address measures that can be undertaken to yield lasting outcomes in order to surmount anxiety.

Engage in Meditation: The practice of meditation serves to quiet and soothe the mind, thereby aiding in the attainment of inner calmness and the alleviation of anxiety. With increased frequency of meditation, one acquires a deeper understanding of managing emotions like anxiety. Could you please explain the process of meditation to me? Merely seek out a serene environment devoid of disturbances, assume a comfortable posture either sitting or standing, gently shut your eyes and attentively observe the rhythm of your breath. Do not attempt to exert control over your breathing, but rather allow it to occur in its most undisturbed and innate state. One can envision a tranquil and serene location of personal affinity, such as a beach or a riverside, and immerse themselves in the olfactory, visual, and auditory sensations it offers. Whenever a distracting thought arises, make a conscious effort to acknowledge it and promptly redirect your focus back to a tranquil state. Engage in this activity for a duration of five minutes, and subsequent to the practice of meditation, it is probable that you will experience a sense of tranquility and composure. Given this mental state, it becomes more manageable to address feelings of anxiety.

Incorporate a Leisure Pursuit: An alternate strategy for mitigating anxiety in the long run involves incorporating a new leisure pursuit. Occasionally, one may experience apprehension due to excessive rigidity in their demeanor. Participating in a pastime is an excellent means of deriving enjoyment. You may engage in gardening, camping, swimming, or any other activity of your choosing. Engaging in an activity that brings you pleasure is likely to alleviate your anxiety and uplift your mood, consequently leading to a heightened enjoyment of life. According to statistical data, individuals who exhibit a more carefree demeanor have a lower propensity to experience anxiety disorders. Therefore, it is advisable to cultivate a mindset that embraces life's unfolding occurrences and observe how such an outlook mitigates anxiety.

Employ Affirmation Technique: Affirmations are constructive declarations one consciously makes to oneself, resulting in significant influence on the subconscious mind. The greater emphasis you place on expressing your confidence and freedom from anxiety, the stronger your belief becomes and the more effectively you alleviate your anxiety. It is essential to incorporate affirmations into your daily routine. Engage in the daily practice of gazing into the looking glass and affirming within yourself the following expressions: 'I possess great competence', 'I possess immense strength', 'I possess the aptitude to flawlessly navigate this circumstance'. By consistently reinforcing these affirmations within your mind, you will gradually internalize them and enhance your self-assurance.

Step 5: Embracing the Present and Maintaining Equanimity Towards the Future

The primary catalyst for anxiety stems from contemplation of the indeterminacy surrounding forthcoming circumstances. By acquiring the ability to dwell in the present moment and relinquish concerns about the future, you can attain a life devoid of anxiety. I understand that you may perceive it to be a simpler task in theory than in practice, however, the following guidelines will facilitate the process of adopting a present-oriented mindset.

Substitute Unrealistic Expectations with Objectives and Strategies: More often than not, our apprehension towards the future arises from maintaining unattainable expectations that inevitably lead us to disappointment. Hence, instead of establishing unattainable aspirations for oneself, it is advisable to establish SMART objectives, as they embody characteristics such as being specific, measurable, achievable, realistic, and timely. Subsequently, make efforts to attain these objectives. You demonstrate greater proficiency in attaining established objectives as opposed to harboring impractical self-expectations. Additionally, engaging in the establishment of goals and conducting preliminary arrangements instills a sense of assurance in the favorable outcome of an upcoming endeavor, thereby mitigating feelings of apprehension and distress.

Embrace Each Day as if it Were Your Final Opportunity: By adopting the practice of cherishing each day as though it were your ultimate chance in life, concerns about the future will be minimized or eradicated entirely. Instead, your attention will be directed towards maximizing the productivity of your day.

Developing Cognitive Influence: We briefly addressed an element of this concept in the preceding section which delved into the subject of meditation. It is imperative for you to acquire the skill of maintaining constant control over your thoughts. The optimal approach to accomplish this is to regulate the flow of thoughts traversing your mind presently. When encountering negative thoughts such as 'I am unable to', 'I will not', 'I ought not to', promptly counter them with affirmative statements such as 'I am capable of', 'I will', 'I should make an attempt'. This will assist you in preventing the cultivation of negativity that can lead to anxiety.

How to Handle Negative Emotions

Once individuals have gained a deeper understanding of various negative emotions, it becomes imperative for them to proceed with acquiring knowledge on effectively managing negative emotions in a constructive manner. Nevertheless, prior to exploring strategies for managing adverse emotions, it is prudent for individuals to grasp the fundamental importance of addressing such negative emotions, thereby increasing their inclination to actively seek solutions for coping with them.

If an individual disregards their emotions, they are essentially repressing their feelings rather than addressing them in the present moment. This approach is considered detrimental to one's well-being as prolonged repression of emotions can lead to their accumulation and eventual uncontrollable release.

On the contrary, it is more advisable to confront the adverse emotion directly, as disregarding it will not result in its cessation. The emotions might manifest themselves unconsciously, obfuscating the individual's awareness of discharging their sentiments onto others. As an illustration, consider a situation where an individual experiences feelings of anger towards their romantic partner, yet wishes to avoid engaging in conflict. In such instances, it is possible for this person to inadvertently direct their anger towards their loved ones and acquaintances, solely due to the residual emotions present within their being as a result of an unrelated relationship. The primary cause for this phenomenon lies in the fact that human emotions serve as indicators to the brain that an individual's current actions or strategies are ineffective.

An illustration of this can be seen in instances where an individual experiences anger or frustration, as the brain is essentially indicating the necessity for a modification in that person's life. If the individual remains unchanged, any circumstance or idea that elicits discomfort within them will continue to serve as a catalyst for the recurrence of those identical thoughts and emotions in subsequent instances.

Furthermore, as previously mentioned, failure to address one's experienced emotions can give rise to detrimental impacts on both their physical and emotional well-being. Nonetheless, fixating on anger and other distressing emotions can result in adverse health effects as well. Hence, it is imperative for individuals to attentively acknowledge their emotions and undertake the requisite actions to effectively release any undesirable emotional states.

Once an individual comprehends the significance of consciously addressing their emotional state, it becomes imperative to delve into a comprehensive understanding of the underlying sensations and sentiments they experience. This implies that individuals will need to introspect and endeavor to identify the circumstances that contribute to the stress and negative emotions experienced in their lives.

Various circumstances can elicit negative emotions, one of which is experiencing an excessively demanding workload. Adverse emotions can also arise from an individual's cognitive processes associated with a specific occurrence. The manner in which an individual perceives and comprehends their experiences has the potential to impact their overall encounter with varied circumstances and determine whether or not they will be susceptible to stress arising from these events.

One of the most pivotal functions fulfilled by a person's emotions is to enable them to discern the presence of underlying issues in their life, thereby facilitating the identification and implementation of requisite alterations.

The subsequent phase involves directing one's attention towards modifiable aspects of an individual's life, while simultaneously reducing focus on those elements that lie beyond their sphere of influence. This implies that individuals must apply the knowledge acquired from their decision-making process in order to effectively handle their emotions. Consequently, individuals will actively explore methods to mitigate the factors that exacerbate their stress, in order to potentially reduce the frequency of negative emotional experiences.

One of the most practical alternatives for individuals to concentrate on harnessing their capacity for change is to mitigate the job-induced stress they experience. This may imply that an individual selectively undertakes a limited workload within their profession, or strategically utilizes their vacation days during periods of heightened stress, such as the holiday season encompassing Christmas or Thanksgiving.

Another approach to effecting the required modifications in one's life is to acquire the skill set of utilizing assertive communication. The objective is for an individual to cease experiencing a sense of being unfairly oppressed by others. This could potentially imply the inclination of an individual to disengage from individuals who exhibit negative speech or behavior towards them, or the development of assertiveness in addressing instances of unfair treatment from others.

Another notable technique is to acquire the skills necessary for altering negative thought patterns through the implementation of cognitive restructuring. This approach entails the process of acknowledging one's flawed cognitive processes, questioning and scrutinizing these thoughts, and ultimately transforming these pessimistic thought patterns into more optimistic ones.

Once an individual has successfully made the necessary alterations within their control, the subsequent stage involves actively seeking a suitable avenue for them. Implementing the required adjustments in one's lifestyle can effectively reduce an individual's adverse emotional states. Nonetheless, it is important to acknowledge that these alterations will not entirely eradicate the stimuli that induce stress. With that being stated, when individuals endeavor to minimize the intensity of their negative emotions, they will likely need to seek out constructive avenues that facilitate the management of those emotions.

Regular physical activity is a commonly sought-after solution by individuals. Physical activity can serve as a source of emotional uplift for individuals, while also serving as a means of catharsis for any adverse emotions an individual may be undergoing.

Meditation serves as an alternative supportive channel as it aids individuals in their endeavor to attain a state of tranquility, particularly in the face of adverse emotions. The objective is to evoke a sense in the individual that the intensity of any negative emotion experienced in that present moment has been significantly diminished.

Additional avenues that could prove advantageous involve actively pursuing opportunities that facilitate personal enjoyment and foster a more jovial atmosphere within one's existence. Increasing opportunities for individuals to experience positive moments in their lives will also facilitate a shift in their outlook on various matters and contribute to the alleviation of their stress.

Having a multitude of positive alternatives available in one's life can diminish the magnitude of negative emotions when they inevitably manifest. It is imperative to consider the options for promoting physical and mental well-being in order to mitigate the impact of adverse emotions on the body and the mind. It might require a certain amount of time to identify the most effective channels for each individual, yet it is a worthwhile endeavor upon discovering the appropriate ones.

When endeavoring to address any emotional situation, it is imperative to bear in one's consciousness additional minor considerations, such as refraining from magnifying or exaggerating circumstances. Ruminating on a matter infused with negative emotions compels an individual to repeatedly replay it in their mind, magnifying its significance beyond reality. As a consequence, it appears considerably more arduous to address the issue.

It is advisable for individuals to cultivate reasonableness, as undesirable emotions can be inevitable. Consequently, it is prudent for them to explore alternative strategies for alleviating such negative sentiments when they inevitably arise. Acquiring the skill of relaxation can prove highly effective in aiding an individual in attaining this objective. Engaging in the activities of reading, taking a leisurely stroll, or engaging in meaningful conversation with a close companion are effective strategies for individuals to attain relaxation in the presence of an unfavorable emotional state.

When addressing adverse emotions, it is equally crucial for individuals to develop an awareness of the impact of these emotions on their well-being, as well as identifying the specific circumstances that serve as catalysts for these negative emotional responses. The objective is for individuals to acquire the skill of proactively planning for adverse emotions, thereby mitigating the extent of their distress.

Another factor to consider when an individual is attempting to manage their emotions is to endeavor to release attachment to their previous experiences. When an individual persistently dwells upon their unfavorable past experiences, they effectively deprive themselves of the ability to fully engage in the present moment as their preoccupation with past grievances impedes their overall well-being.

Medical Conditions Which Contribute to the Development of Anxiety

Prior to reaching the conclusion that your anxiety is rooted in your psychological issues or high levels of stress, it is imperative to assess your overall physical well-being. Frequently, individuals may encounter challenges in managing panic attacks or various forms of anxiety, as an underlying health condition, which may go unnoticed or unrecognized, can serve as a catalyst for these symptoms, intensifying feelings of anxiousness.

However, it must be acknowledged that anxiety does not always manifest as an isolated mental health concern. It can also serve as the principal indication of a significant medical condition necessitating specialized medical intervention. Upon receiving treatment for this condition, you will substantially increase your prospects of eradicating anxiety from your existence.

Numerous investigations and comprehensive analyses undertaken by experts have led to the consensus that anxiety is indicative of the aforementioned ailments and medical conditions:

1. Cardiovascular disorders Cardiovascular ailments Cardiovascular conditions Diseases related to the cardiovascular system

Anxiety is widely acknowledged as being among the primary indicators of a myocardial infarction. Myocardial infarctions and anxiety episodes may exhibit comparable symptoms, including thoracic discomfort, accelerated heart rate, dyspnea, perspiration, and panic attacks. Cardiac rhythm disturbances or arrhythmias can result in episodes of tachycardia accompanied by heightened levels of anxiety. Cardiovascular conditions including heart failure, angina, and valvular disease bear significant potential in exacerbating panic attacks.

2. Lung disease

Respiratory disorders wherein individuals face challenges in acquiring sufficient oxygen can exhibit a correlation with pronounced anxiety. Both chronic obstructive pulmonary disease and asthma induce considerable anxiety as individuals experience difficulty obtaining sufficient oxygen due to unresponsive airways.

Pulmonary embolism is a perilous medical condition that manifests as the presence of a blood clot, which migrates to the pulmonary system resulting in impaired gas exchange within the lungs. The most salient indicators manifesting in individuals include feelings of anxiety and an accelerated heart rate.

3. Carcinoid tumors

This condition is a result of the activity of hormone-secreting cells located within the glands of the intestine. Carcinoid tumors produce diverse hormones, including a significant neurotransmitter called serotonin. Excessive levels of serotonin in the bloodstream frequently give rise to carcinoid syndrome, characterized by symptoms including elevated heart rate, heightened anxiety, frequent episodes of diarrhoea, and sudden reddening of the skin.

4. Pheochromocytoma

This is a neoplastic growth that triggers an excessive secretion of adrenaline, irrespective of the physiological demand for it. In addition to the anxiety manifested as panic attacks, pheochromocytoma may induce symptoms such as headaches, palpitations, hypertension, and excessive perspiration. The occurrence of a panic attack in this instance is commonly accompanied by a pallid complexion.

5. Hyperthyroidism

When the thyroid gland exhibits excessive activity, it results in heightened metabolic rates and manifests symptoms including anxiety, increased heart rate, and substantial weight loss. If not addressed, this condition has the potential to induce severe episodes of panic.

If you do not exhibit any of these aforementioned health conditions, it becomes more feasible to effectively cope with your anxiety and mitigate the frequency of your relentless episodes of panic. Nonetheless, the foundation lies in personal learning, and the subsequent section will provide assistance in this regard.

Four: Profound Epiphanies Regarding Panic Episodes

Isabel Allende once eloquently expressed, "The inevitability of fear is a truth I must acknowledge, yet I refuse to allow it to immobilize me."

Her words resonated deeply with me. Fear is an inherent human response, and it is within your jurisdiction to determine whether you grant it dominion over you or establish complete mastery over it. Panic episodes invariably entail profound apprehension, generating a sense of captivity and helplessness, rendering individuals too feeble and intimidated to regulate the circumstances.

In actuality, panic attacks do not manifest with the same level of fear and intensity that one might perceive. They may constitute an integral part of your life and possess the potential to facilitate advancements in specific domains, provided that you acquire further knowledge about them. Presented here are profound insights regarding panic attacks that have the potential to significantly alter your perception of them, enabling a more optimistic outlook.

Apprehensions do not serve as debilitating extraterrestrial organisms

Similar to any individual who experiences anxiety, you perceive your fears as formidable adversaries. It is evident that they serve to incapacitate individuals, impeding their progress towards personal aspirations and ambitions. In reality, apprehension does not equate to an adversary.

Regardless of the number of books you read or self-help courses you pursue, the eradication of your fears will only be possible when you come to the realization that they do not pose as adversaries.

Rather than viewing your fear as a debilitating, agonizing, and intimidating adversary, consider it to be a constructive bodily reaction to the circumstances you find yourself in. Apprehension can manifest in both pathological and beneficial forms, with the latter being a vital physiological response that enhances one's ability to navigate challenging circumstances and ensure survival.

In instances of perilous circumstances, the secretion of adrenaline and other formidable hormones induces acceleration in heart rates and breathing. When your muscles experience tension, there is an increase in your blood pressure, resulting in the redirection of blood flow to the brain, legs, and arms. The human body undergoes physiological changes in preparation for either a defensive response or an aggressive response, whereby it is primed to either escape from a perceived threat or confront it directly.

An appropriate reaction to fear can be brief unless an individual has a negative tendency to excessively analyze each aspect of the perilous circumstance. It tranquillizes until the subsequent circumstance rekindles it. Numerous individuals interpret this innate fear reaction as a manifestation of panic, thus exacerbating its intensity through excessive rumination and the contemplation of adverse outcomes.

The state of being apprehensive escalates to a pathological level when it is elicited by innocuous occurrences, for instance, embarking on a journey, establishing acquaintances, or partaking in a festive gathering. In this instance, a panic attack arises as an unconscious response to your triggering.

The manifestation of your pathological fear can be attributed to your diminished sense of self-value.

In the majority of instances, your experience of panic attacks and anxiety can be attributed to a direct correlation with your diminished sense of self-worth or the lack thereof. Ultimately, when one's self-esteem is diminished, the world can be perceived as a harsh and inequitable environment.

At a subconscious level, you undoubtedly hold the belief that happiness has no place within the confines of your existence. You consistently anticipate and facilitate the occurrence of disasters. You are apprehensive about the future due to the lingering impact of past, devastating events.

Each day, you experience the weight of expectation to excel, exceed, and attain flawlessness due to a sense of inadequacy in earning the respect and affection of others. One might choose to refrain from attending meetings or Friday office gatherings due to apprehension about colleagues' potential lack of enthusiasm for their company. You underestimate your capabilities, diminish your skills, and socially distance yourself due to your diminished self-confidence that elicits feelings of anxiety and bouts of panic.

You exhibit skepticism towards your decisions and lack confidence in yourself, thereby permitting your fear to engender adverse outcomes. When encountering something novel, one experiences a sense of immobilization due to apprehension regarding any potential alterations.

Consequently, you experience feelings of confinement, anxiety, excessive burden, and confusion. You view your entire existence as a constant source of distress, wherein anxiety and fear have ingrained themselves as enduring facets of your being.

Enhancing one's self-esteem can mitigate the possibility of

experiencing panic attacks and reduce the adverse consequences of anxiety. Hence, I implore you to comprehend the inherent value that resides within you.

While you may encounter challenges in forging new friendships, and your social skills may not be impeccable, it is crucial to acknowledge your inherent value as an individual. Even in the event of not obtaining your desired employment, you retain inherent value. External factors do not exert any influence on your intrinsic value; it originates from within your psyche and your acceptance of oneself.

Enhancing your self-esteem will facilitate the effective management of apprehension and distress, while preserving your overall sense of welfare and contentment. Continuously reiterate the affirmation, "I am deserving," until you genuinely internalize this belief.

You are filled with apprehension at the mere thought of fear.

Despite the multitude of triggers associated with anxiety disorders, it is often the fear itself and its potential consequences that instill profound dread. Managing a panic attack can be an immensely distressing experience - the constriction of the chest, the difficulty in breathing, and the irregular heartbeats instill the belief that imminent death is inevitable and inescapable.

This is the reason behind your avoidance of triggering situations that cause panic in you. You cease formulating ambitious aspirations for the future, curtail social engagements, adhere to your customary regimen, and remain within the confines of your comfort zone. One's ruminations persistently revolve around apprehensions and feasible strategies to circumvent them. One acquires the knowledge of coexisting with them and employs all available means to prevent the occurrence of panic attacks.

However, the issue lies in the fact that when the primary cause of distress is one's own existence, it results in a severe limitation on living according to one's desires.

As you confront your fear, it becomes more potent.

Engaging in extensive endeavors and devoting significant time towards the elimination of fear from your existence may inadvertently exacerbate the situation. Not all fears are able to be permanently conquered. Apprehensions have a tendency to protect themselves, thereby facilitating the exacerbation of panic attacks in terms of their intensity and frequency.

You may exhaust your mental faculties exploring novel approaches to confront anxiety, testing myriad strategies and methodologies aimed at mitigating its detrimental effects on your well-being. However, ultimately experiencing a sense of profound inadequacy. The utilization of such tactics and techniques may elicit an exponential growth in fear due to an excessive preoccupation with them.

Your fear becomes the focal point around which your entire life revolves. Your focus is predominantly directed towards your fear and the strategies employed to combat it, consequently leading to an unconscious amplification of the fear itself.

Befriend your fear

I am cognizant of what may be occupying your thoughts at present—namely, the question of whether I have lost my sanity. What strategies can I employ to establish a harmonious relationship with my fear and anxiety? It may seem unconventional or illogical, but it is indeed possible to cultivate a friendship with these emotions. Assign a designation to the entity and allocate a brief portion of your daily routine to engage in verbal communication with said entity.

Genuinely attend to its concerns and reassure your apprehension that favorable outcomes are assured. Whenever your fear arises, engage in conversation with it to communicate your presence and support. Your apprehension may suggest that the present moment is unfavorable for embarking on a new relationship; nevertheless, endeavor to assuage these concerns by acknowledging that it is indeed an opportune time to do so.

The key is to regard your fear as your closest ally. Do you consistently provide them with beneficial advice? Your fear could benefit from some useful guidance. Regardless of whether you choose to vocalize your thoughts to your fear or not, it is highly probable that it will be receptive to your communication. Please ensure that you communicate in a composed and assured manner.

By assigning a name to your fear, you will cease to associate your identity with it. You will no longer be subjected to apprehension, as you are aware of the existence of an autonomous entity harboring concerns, uncertainties, and vulnerabilities. Your responsibility is to assist this individual in managing their anxiety.

It is possible that it will require a period of several weeks or possibly even months in order for you to assist your fear in acquiring increased self-assurance and beginning to lead an independent existence. However, I assure you that afterwards, you will not receive any further communication regarding this matter. You will commence experiencing life in a liberated manner, on your own accord. You will experience a sense of liberation and contentment at last.

Making Friends

The cultivation of friendships becomes a desirable endeavor when we place importance on the gratification derived from companionship. The majority of individuals possess only a limited number of friends in whom they place complete trust regarding their deepest emotions and confidential matters. When one bestows their companionship upon another, it assumes a vital role within the context of a relationship. Regrettably, numerous individuals experience a sense of isolation, lacking an individual they can confide in and consider a trusted companion. This phenomenon is subject to change, as the inception of strong friendships is possible at any phase of one's lifetime.

It has been commonly expressed that love possesses an innate capability to overlook flaws, while friendship is primarily characterized by its tendency to remain oblivious to imperfections. Companions can serve as confidants, advocates, or empathizers who provide motivation, constructive criticism, sincere perspectives, and typically extensive guidance. We disclose certain information to our friends that we would not disclose to any other individuals. A trusted confidant is an individual with whom you can impart sensitive information, assured that they will not harbor any ill will towards you. They are also someone who possesses shared interests and experiences, enhancing one's overall sense of satisfaction and contentment.

Establishing relationships requires a considerable investment of time, exertion, dedication, reciprocity, and a substantial degree of acceptance towards the inherent fallibility that exists within all human beings.

The establishment and maintenance of friendships are predicated upon four fundamental principles.

• Assume the initiative and make contact with others. • Display authentic curiosity in individuals.

• Practice interpersonal decorum and exhibit benevolence towards others. • Recognize and appreciate the inherent worth and contributions of both yourself and others as distinct individuals with valuable qualities and capabilities. While many individuals are receptive to forming new relationships, their focus often shifts towards important life endeavors such as professional advancement and building a family. Certain individuals hold the view that the process of cultivating friendships demands a substantial amount of time and exertion.

Cultivating Mutual Trust is another rationale for the time it takes to establish friendships, as Trust necessitates a gradual development process. In order to establish trust with an individual, it is necessary to disclose personal information and emotions, enabling the other party to develop an authentic understanding of your character and areas of sensitivity. Over the course of time, you and your friends will increasingly divulge personal information, fostering a deepening Trust between you. During the nascent phases of a friendship, individuals may encounter uncertainty regarding the appropriate level of self-disclosure. If you possess an understanding of the equilibrium of information exchanged, it is likely that your level of personal revelation will be suited to the circumstances. The establishment of unwavering trust in an individual's integrity and dependability demands a significant investment of time, whereas a single violation of that trust has the potential to swiftly dismantle a relationship. When an individual demonstrates their trust in you and shares their inner thoughts or secrets, it is crucial to not betray their trust and compromise the faith and confidence they have placed in you.

To Engage in Social Interactions, Frequent Enjoyable Environments
There exists a multitude of venues conducive to meeting individuals, with the understanding that certain places offer superior opportunities, particularly in fostering connections with someone of significance. The appropriate location can encompass a range of settings such as a social gathering, religious assembly, political assembly, or even a formal educational session for adults. If you possess a shared interest, this is the appropriate location for you. When

individuals encounter one another at a location where their shared interests align, a mutual basis is established, facilitating the initiation of a friendship.

Meaningful connections can be forged in unexpected places. Consider the individuals you encounter and perceive within your professional environment, residential area, and notably during leisure or communal gatherings you partake in. There exist numerous individuals who have the potential to become your friends, and it is possible to establish relationships with them.

Establishing Acquaintance with Individuals Upon encountering consistent interactions with the same individuals over an extended period, one can engage in initial conversations. Determine whether there are shared interests or similarities and, if favorable circumstances allow, commence the establishment of a friendship. Developing acquaintanceship with individuals you frequently encounter shall facilitate the aforementioned task. Commence by initiating a cordial and amiable greeting, accompanied by a pleasant smile. In the event that an occasion presents itself, proceed to formally introduce your person to others.

Maintain a cordial atmosphere—Avoid delving into deep or grave topics. Once you have exchanged greetings multiple times, there is a good chance you will encounter an occasion to pause and engage in brief conversation. Perhaps it can be encountered within the workplace, while strolling along a thoroughfare, or within a nearby grocery establishment. Demonstrate a genuine desire to further acquaint yourself with the individual by initiating and participating in light-hearted dialogue. It is not necessary to express profound or exceedingly impressive ideas. It would be more advantageous to adopt an informal demeanor characterized by friendliness and openness. Please bear in mind that engaging in casual conversation conveys the message of genuine interest and willingness to engage in meaningful dialogue. Let\\\'s talk!\\\"

Employ Ritual Inquiries to Convey the Notion: \\\"I Seek to Acquire a Deeper Understanding of Your Background\\\" What is your tenure within this organization? May I inquire as to the length of time you have resided in this local area? What was your previous place of residence? What factors led to your involvement in this line of work? May I inquire about the leisure activities that you partake in within this vicinity?

These formal inquiries serve as an indication of your curiosity and provide the other party with an opportunity to reciprocate their curiosity towards you. Attentively observe the speaker's discourse to identify valuable pieces of information and take note of pertinent subjects. Pose the question to oneself: "Do I aspire to establish a deeper acquaintance with this individual?"

www.ingramcontent.com/pod-product-compliance
Lightning Source LLC
Chambersburg PA
CBHW050237120526
44590CB00016B/2126